# ESTABLISHED
## IN THE FAITH

## 12 Conversations to Lead Your Child to Profess Faith in Christ

D1547600

## By John C. Kwasny, PhD

**CDM's *Established* series**

© PCA Christian Discipleship Ministries

PCA Committee on Discipleship Ministries
1700 North Brown Road, Suite 102 Lawrenceville, Georgia 30043
Bookstore: 678.825.1100 | www.pcabookstore.com

ISBN: 978-1-944964-18-4

Dedicated to all *our covenant children*

# ESTABLISHED IN THE FAITH
## USING THIS MANUAL

One of the prime responsibilities of all Christian parents is to give testimony of their faith, by their words and actions, to the next generation. Teaching children the gospel of salvation that is found in Christ alone, through faith alone, by the grace of God alone is never to be neglected or left to someone else. Yet many parents today find it difficult to have these faith-filled conversations, or just don't know where to start. This manual provides a solid biblical and theologically reformed approach to these talks between parent and child.

The content of this manual is applicable for children of all ages, whenever a child is ready for gospel conversations. Yet it is especially geared for children between the ages of seven to ten, due to the desire to lead a child to profess faith in Christ as early as possible. (*Children and adults with cognitive disabilities will also greatly benefit from this discussion guide.*) **Each conversation is divided into four sections:**

 DIGGING IN

The *Digging In* section gets the parent-child conversation started with icebreaker-type questions. It serves as a way to introduce the topic and get your child talking.

 DEFINING TERMS

Conversations with our children about the gospel of Jesus Christ demands some essential definition work. The Defining Terms section is a brief, interactive way to make sure your child understands some of the foundational words/phrases of the faith. Show them the importance of knowing what our words actually mean!

DISCUSSING TOGETHER

Then, it's time for the main portion of the conversation with your child–the *Discussing Together* section. In a discussion format, parent and child can talk through each part of the gospel that is essential for a profession of faith. All sections of Scripture given in each conversation are from the *English Standard Version (ESV)*.

In order to personalize these conversations with your child, a *Detail your Story* section is typically included. This is the place for a parent to share his or her own testimony of faith along the way.

 DECLARING THE TRUTH

Each conversation closes out where it should, with the active professing of a portion of the faith. This allows a parent to lead his or her child to put together what is to be believed about God, ourselves, our problem, and the only solution to that problem.

The goal of this last section is to produce a heartfelt and thoughtful profession of faith in Jesus Christ. This is not just a script to be robotically repeated, but a Biblical guide to personalize and accept as true.

**Enjoy having these "establishing the faith" conversations with your child.** Whether your church encourages children to become communing members at a younger age, or you desire to prepare your child for a communicant's class which comes later, these talks are vital to the work of redemption in Jesus Christ!

# Table of Contents

USING THIS MANUAL: ..................................................5

CONVERSATION 1:  **God is...** ...................................9

CONVERSATION 2:  **God's Law is...** ....................... 15

CONVERSATION 3:  **The World is...**......................... 21

CONVERSATION 4:  **I am...**..................................... 27

CONVERSATION 5:  **Jesus is...**............................... 33

CONVERSATION 6:  **Jesus lived...** ......................... 39

CONVERSATION 7:  **Jesus died...** .......................... 45

CONVERSATION 8:  **My life is...**............................. 51

CONVERSATION 9:  **The Holy Spirit is...**............... 57

CONVERSATION 10: **The Church is...** .................... 63

CONVERSATION 11: **The Lord's Supper is...** ..........69

CONVERSATION 12: **The Future is...** ..................... 75

# ESTABLISHED IN THE FAITH
## CONVERSATION 1

# God is...

## DIGGING IN

Do you believe that I am your parent? Why? **(Allow answers.)** Maybe you believe it because I have told you I am your parent. Or, maybe, you believe it because you see that we look alike. Or, maybe, you have looked at baby pictures with me holding you. The good news is that what you believe is TRUE! I am your parent!

So, what does it mean to BELIEVE?

## DEFINING TERMS

The sort of BELIEVING that we need to talk about has two parts to it. First, believing is AGREEING that something is true.

> **So, let's try this part out:** Do you agree that, as a human being, eating is necessary for survival? [Yes] Good! This is a proven fact!

But then, there is an important second part to BELIEVING. Believing includes COMMITTING your life to that truth. It means there is always a DOING part to this sort of belief.

> **Let's try this part out:** What if you AGREED that eating is necessary for survival, but decided never to eat again? Would this be true belief? No way!

Do you get it? To believe means to AGREE something is true and to ACT appropriately upon it.

# DISCUSSING TOGETHER

What, then, is the first thing you need to BELIEVE? Some would say you have to believe in YOURSELF. But is that right? No! We must first believe that…

# *God is…*

Do you know that there are many people who believe that GOD ISN'T? They believe that God is a fairytale or just a made-up story. So, how can you and I be sure that God IS? First, we know that God exists by paying attention to the world around us. In other words, by understanding that…

## *God shows us Himself in Creation.*

### Read Romans 1:19-20.

**[19] For what can be known about God is plain to them, because God has shown it to them. [20] For his invisible attributes, namely, his eternal power and divine nature, have been clearly perceived, ever since the creation of the world, in the things that have been made…**

Do you hear that? We can know that God exists by looking at this amazing world in which we live. Think about it: Have you ever seen incredible animals that fascinate you? Which ones? **(Allow answers.)**

What about beautiful plants, or high mountains, or tall trees, or deep oceans, or far-away stars? How can we truly see the creation all around us and not believe that GOD IS? This world is awesome in so many ways.

But we have been given something even better to teach us that God exists. It is something that also tells us who God is, what God does, and how we are to respond to Him. Do you know what that is? **(Allow answers.)**

## *God shows us Himself in the Bible.*

*Do you know how the Bible begins?* **Read Genesis 1:1.**

### [1] In the beginning, God created the heavens and the earth.

This one verse tells us a couple of important things about God, doesn't it? It tells us He exists. It also tells us that He created the universe. And, even better, these first words are only the beginning of a whole lot of information about who God is!

The Bible tells us the truth about who God is. Without it, we would just be guessing about God's identity, wouldn't we? We would be tempted to fill in the "God is..." blank with our own opinions, such as:

**God is...just a human with superpowers.**
**Or, God is...a being who doesn't know everything.**
**Or, God is...limited, and not all-powerful.**

Unfortunately, people who deny the truth of the Bible end up making God in their own image, if they believe God even exists. Then, they form their beliefs about God around their own ideas. Does that sound wise to you?

Hopefully, you understand that the only right and safe way to know the truth about God is to take it from God's Word. It is God alone who shows us who He is. So, it is essential that you learn ALL of God's Word!

## *Detail your story...*

**Tell your child about the first person who taught you about God. Also share what you first thought about God— either truth or error.**

So, among all the marvelous things the Bible says about God, where should we begin? Let's just touch on five for today.

### God is Infinite and Eternal.

That means God has no beginning and no end. He has always been and will always be. Do you believe that?

**Read Revelation 1:8.**

**8 "I am the Alpha and the Omega," says the Lord God, "who is and who was and who is to come, the Almighty."**

### God is One God, in Three Persons.

We believe in the One, true and living God.

**Read Deuteronomy 6:4.**

⁴ **Hear, O Israel: The LORD our God, the LORD is one.**

Yet, this ONE God is a TRIUNE God. That means He is three persons–God the Father, God the Son, and God the Holy Spirit. While the TRINITY is hard to understand, God's Word teaches it over and over again. Such as when Jesus says these words of Himself...

**Read John 10:30.**

³⁰ **I and the Father are one.**

We'll have conversations about Jesus and the Holy Spirit later on.

## *God is the Creator and Sustainer.*

We already saw this in Genesis 1:1, didn't we? The first few chapters of the Bible teach us that God created ALL THINGS. And then, Paul wrote this further truth about the Son of God:

**Read Colossians 1:17.**

¹⁷ **And he is before all things, and in him all things hold together.**

## *God is Sovereign.*

That means He is the Almighty King of the universe, and in total control of all things. To be sovereign is to be in complete charge of everything.

**Read Psalm 115:3.**

³ **Our God is in the heavens; he does all that he pleases.**

## *God is Holy.*

This final description of who God is will lead us into our next conversation. It means that God is perfect, completely righteous, and totally set apart from sinful human beings.

**Read Isaiah 6:3.**

³ **And one called to another and said: "Holy, holy, holy is the LORD of hosts; the whole earth is full of his glory!"**

# DECLARING THE TRUTH

*Lead your child to begin to profess the faith in his or her words:*

## *I believe that God is...*

- the God who is clearly shown in Creation and the Bible.
- infinite and eternal.
- one God in three persons.
- the Creator and Sustainer of the universe.
- sovereign.
- perfectly Holy.

*We will add to our profession of the faith, our declaration of the truth, when we talk next time...*

# ESTABLISHED IN THE FAITH
## CONVERSATION *2*

# God's law is...

## DIGGING IN

Do we have rules in our family? Of course we do! A family cannot function properly without rules. But I'm sure that we have rules that you either don't like very much, or find hard to obey. Can you tell me one of those? **(Allow answers.)** Sometimes obeying the rules is a very difficult thing.

Another word we use for "rule" is LAW. Countries, states, and cities all have LAWS, don't they? We need to talk about a different (but similar) set of LAWS today...

## DEFINING TERMS

Where do we find out about GOD'S LAW? That's right, in the Bible. We can find the LAW OF GOD all through the pages of Scripture, from Genesis to Revelation. There were several types of LAWS given to Israel and to us today.

The specific LAWS that we need to discuss are called God's MORAL LAW. His moral law are those rules on how we are to live as children of God—members of God's Kingdom. This LAW is what God expects His people to do and to be.

The main list of God's MORAL law is known as the Ten Commandments. Can you tell me some (or all) of those? **(Help your child recite the Ten Commandments.)** Do you hear how these are RULES on how to live before God and with one another? So, when we speak of God's LAW we are speaking of His MORAL LAW.

# DISCUSSING TOGETHER

If we believe that GOD IS, we then need to know how He relates to His people. As we just said, God has given His people something very important: His LAW. Just as our rules define the way we live together as a family, God's LAW shows us how His children are to live. So let's spend a few minutes discussing what:

# God's Law is...

My rules tell you something about what is important to me. If I make a rule for you to never jump on the couch, it's probably because I don't want the furniture ruined, right? Well, that leads us to our first point about God's Law:

## God's Law reflects God's character.

It tells us what God is like! For example, when God says, "Do not murder," it shows us that God is a God of LIFE! He values human life because we are made in the image of God. All of God's LAW teaches us about who God is and what He expects from all His creation. This means that we must then also believe that...

## God's Law is perfect.

Listen to Psalm 19. **Read Psalm 19:7.**

> **7 The law of the LORD is perfect, reviving the soul; the testimony of the LORD is sure, making wise the simple;**

That makes sense, doesn't it? If God is perfect, then His LAW must be perfect too! Is that how you think about God's LAW? Unfortunately, many people believe that there is something wrong with God's LAW – that it's too strict, or too narrow, or too harsh. But that would mean that God is too strict, too narrow, or too harsh. Is that right? No way!

The rules I give you aren't always perfect because I am not perfect. The laws of our country aren't perfect because they are made by imperfect people. But ALL of the laws of God are perfect because we know He is perfect!

## God's Law is the standard of right and wrong.

Why is stealing wrong? **(Allow answers.)** It certainly upsets people who lose their possessions. But it is wrong because God says it is wrong! He protects our things from thieves by declaring that stealing is against His character.

Why is lying wrong? **(Allow answers.)** No one likes to be lied to, right? But it is not people who determine that lying is wrong–it's God. Since He is TRUTH, He determined that lying is wrong. Again, it goes against His character!

Why is disobeying your parents wrong? Did a bunch of adults just make up that law? No way! God says it's wrong since it goes against His structure of authority. To disobey parents is to disobey God, our Father!

Do you get it? God's LAW is the standard for what is right and what is wrong. That means it doesn't matter if YOU think a "little" lie is okay–it's wrong because God says so!

Listen to this verse. **Read Romans 7:7.**

**⁷...Yet if it had not been for the law, I would not have known sin. For I would not have known what it is to covet if the law had not said, "You shall not covet."**

And this one. **Read Romans 7:12.**

**¹²So the law is holy, and the commandment is holy and righteous and good.**

So we know what is right and wrong because God gave us His LAW. God's LAW is holy and good!

## God's Law is a teacher.

What does a teacher do? That's easy – he teaches! And what is the student supposed to do? Learn! So what does God's Law teach us that we must learn?

**Read Romans 3:20.**

**²⁰For by works of the law no human being will be justified in his sight, since through the law comes knowledge of sin.**

It teaches us that we are sinners. It teaches us that we cannot save ourselves. It teaches us that only God is righteous. We learn who God is, and who we are, through His LAW!

Then, there's this verse. **Read Galatians 3:24.**

**²⁴ So then, the law was our guardian until Christ came, in order that we might be justified by faith.**

We will talk more about this verse in a future conversation. The word "guardian" can also be translated "tutor" or "teacher." God's LAW keeps us, so that Jesus can save us from our law-breaking ways. The law can teach us our sin, but cannot save us from our sin.

---

# *Detail your story...*
**Talk to your child about how God's Law has shown you more of God's holiness, as well as your own sinfulness.**

---

## God's Law is to be obeyed.

This should be obvious, right? The Ten Commandments are not named the "Ten Suggestions," are they? God's MORAL LAW is our rule of life. God requires all people to obey His MORAL LAW.

**Read Ecclesiastes 12:13.**

**¹³ The end of the matter; all has been heard. Fear God and keep his commandments, for this is the whole duty of man.**

Do you know that you have a duty to obey ALL of God's LAW? It is not optional! You and I cannot pick and choose which commands to obey and which commands to ignore. All of God's LAW must be obeyed.

But that leaves us with several questions for our upcoming conversations, such as:

**Can we actually obey God's Law?**

**Is it possible to obey ALL of God's Law?**

**What happens if we disobey God's Law?**

Until next time...

# DECLARING THE TRUTH

*Lead your child to continue to profess the faith in his or her words:*

## I believe that God's law is...

- God's holy character.
- perfect.
- the standard for right and wrong.
- instructive about God.
- instructive about our sin.
- to be obeyed.

*We will add to our profession of the faith, our declaration of the truth, when we talk next time...*

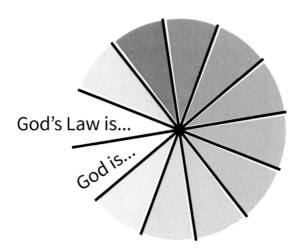

# ESTABLISHED IN THE FAITH
## CONVERSATION *3*

# The World is...

 ## DIGGING IN

Here's a question for you: Do you live in the WORLD? **(Allow answers.)** Of course you do! Every person who is alive lives in the WORLD, right?

So, who created the WORLD, and everything in it? **(Allow answers.)** Do you know that some people think that the WORLD just came to be, all on its own? But God's Word tells us the truth – that God created the WORLD! Let's talk more about that together...

 ## DEFINING TERMS

So, the WORLD is the place God created for all His creation to live. It is our big, round planet earth! But there are a couple of other important uses of this word that you need to know.

Sometimes, we use the word WORLD just to describe the PEOPLE who live on earth. When the Bible says, "God so loved the WORLD..." it means that God loves PEOPLE, not just the PLANET.

A third meaning of WORLD is all the people who do not love Jesus. This is the WORLD that is fighting against God and doing WORLDLY (sinful) things. Why don't you want to be part of that WORLD? **(Allow answers.)** We can either love the sinful things of the WORLD, or the righteous things of God! As we talk some more, I will help you remember the different ways we talk about the WORLD.

# DISCUSSING TOGETHER

First, we believe that GOD IS, right? He is our infinite, eternal, One God in three persons, Creator of all things. Then, we also believe that He gave us His LAW to obey, to show us His holiness, to teach us right from wrong, and to show us our need for a Savior. Now, let's think about what we believe…

# *The World is…*

Do you think the WORLD is a pretty neat place to live? I do! There is so much to see, so much to do--so much beauty on display everywhere you look. The world is filled with amazing mountains and jungles, oceans and beaches, people and cultures. What do you like most about the world? **(Allow answers.)** So, here's our first thing to believe about the WORLD…

## *God created and sustains the world.*

**Read Psalm 24:1-2.**

> **¹ The earth is the LORD's and the fullness thereof, the world and those who dwell therein, ₂ for he has founded it upon the seas and established it upon the rivers.**

We already know this, right? The WORLD and all who live in this WORLD is the LORD's. He created all things. We learn this truth from the very beginning of the Bible, don't we? The WORLD did not just come into being on its own – God made it. So that means God is the King and the Owner of the entire WORLD!

But as you are growing up in this WORLD, are you also seeing that there are lots of problems all around you? People hurt other people. Disease and illness lead to death of family and friends. Scary things like hurricanes, blizzards, and violent storms destroy the world every day. Nations go to war, droughts kill crops, and people suffer in so many ways. This teaches us the truth that…

## *We all live in a fallen world.*

What does that mean? Here's an important verse that tells us the problem.

**Read Romans 5:12-13.**

¹² Therefore, just as sin came into the world through one man, and death through sin, and so death spread to all men because all sinned— ¹³ for sin indeed was in the world before the law was given, but sin is not counted where there is no law.

What came into the world? Sin did! What did sin cause to also come into the world? Death! This is what we mean when we describe the world as FALLEN. It has fallen into sin, since all people are sinners. It has become a place of death because sin brings death. But then, there is more bad news...

## The world is under the power of Satan.

Listen to this. **Read I John 5:19.**

¹⁹ We know that we are from God, and the whole world lies in the power of the evil one.

Now, we have to be careful here. Does this mean that Satan (the evil one) is in control of God's WORLD? No way! But, we must know that Satan does have power over people in the world who reject God. How does Satan have power over worldly people? **(Allow answers.)** Satan lies to them, and they believe it. Satan tempts them, and they sin. Satan accuses them, and they agree with him. Satan attempts to eat them alive like a lion tries to devour an antelope. The world lies in the power of the evil one!

So, all those who live under the power of Satan are truly WORLDLY people. But you and I can also be influenced by the things of this WORLD. Therefore, we need to also understand this next truth...

## God calls us not to love the things of this world.

Listen to God's Word again. **Read I John 2:15-16.**

¹⁵ Do not love the world or the things in the world. If anyone loves the world, the love of the Father is not in him. ¹⁶ For all that is in the world—the desires of the flesh and the desires of the eyes and pride of life—is not from the Father but is from the world.

Do you hear that? God tells His people over and over again not to fall in love with the sinful ways of this world. We always have two choices: To either love God or love the WORLD. The world is all about pride and selfishness. That isn't God's way, is it? God is all about righteousness and holiness.

---

## *Detail your story...*

**Talk to your child about specific ways that the world is influencing him or her to sin. Include an example from your own life.**

---

Then, there is one more important truth about the WORLD, which will lead us into more conversations.

### God so loved the world!

Do you know this verse already? **Read John 3:16.**

**16 For God so loved the world, that he gave his only Son, that whoever believes in him should not perish but have eternal life.**

Does this wonderful verse say that God loves the WORLDLY things of this WORLD? No way! Does He love the sin and death of this WORLD? No again. What God loves is SINNERS. He loves His people who are caught in the clutches of sin. And, He loves ALL types of people all over this great big WORLD of ours.

Listen to this last verse. **Read I John 4:4.**

**4 Little children, you are from God and have overcome them, for he who is in you is greater than he who is in the world.**

God's love for His people is greater than the sinful power of the evil one in this world. But, you must be His child in order to overcome this world! That's a topic for another conversation...

# DECLARING THE TRUTH

*Lead your child to begin to profess
the faith in his or her words:*

## I believe the World is…

- created and sustained by God.
- fallen and sinful.
- under the power of the evil one.
- not to be loved by God's people.
- full of people loved by God!

We will add to our profession of the faith, our declaration of the truth, when we talk again next time…

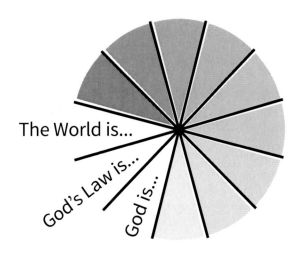

# ESTABLISHED IN THE FAITH
## CONVERSATION 4

# I am...

 ## DIGGING IN

If someone walked up to you at church and said, "Who are you?" what would you say? **(Allow answers.)** You would probably start by saying your name, right?

But after stating your name, how would you describe yourself to a person who doesn't know you? Would you talk about how you look, how old you are, and who your parents are? Maybe you would even talk about the things you like to do, or what you want to be when you grow up.

 ## DEFINING TERMS

What we are talking about today has to do with the term IDENTITY. Have you heard of that word? There are several definitions of IDENTITY, but here's the one for our conversation: **An IDENTITY is the unique character or personality of an individual.** In other words, your IDENTITY describes who you really are.

So, what is special about you? Or maybe a better question is: What is special about ALL people? Are we just the same as animals? Are we exactly like God? Or, do we have an IDENTITY that simply separates us from all the rest of God's creation?

We need to talk about your IDENTITY today. You may be surprised at WHO YOU ARE!

 # DISCUSSING TOGETHER

Last time, we had a great conversation about the WORLD. Who created and sustains the WORLD? [God.] What kind of WORLD do we live in? [A fallen world.] What is the best news for this WORLD? [God so loved the world.] Do you live in this WORLD? Yes, you do! So, let's talk about YOU. In other words, who...

# *I am...*

Remember, this is your IDENTITY! You need to know WHO YOU ARE. We will start from the beginning.

## *I am made in God's image.*

### Read Genesis 1:27.

**27 So God created man in his own image, in the image of God he created him; male and female he created them.**

This is what happened at the beginning, isn't it? God created man in his own IMAGE. That means ALL people are made in God's IMAGE, not just our first parents. So what is an IMAGE? **(Allow answers.)** An IMAGE is a likeness, a representation of something else.

Do you see what that means? You were made to be like God! So what is God like? **(Allow answers.)** We were created to love, to show kindness, to think, to be righteous, to be holy, to be strong, to be merciful. There is a long list of God's qualities, right?

So does that mean you can be EXACTLY like God? No way! You have a body, and God doesn't. God knows all things, and you don't. God is perfect, and you aren't. People are created to be like God and have certain qualities that make us unique as His creations. That leads us to the next truth...

## *I am a human being.*

I hope you already know that you are not an animal. You are not an angel either. And you certainly aren't God. As a human being, you are one of God's creatures. As we just said, you are a unique and special creature, but still just one of God's creation.

Recognizing that you are a human being also means you know that you are made of dust. What does that mean? **(Allow answers.)** It means that you have a body that gets sick, gets hungry, and even will die one day. God created you as BODY and SOUL. You have a forever soul, but you have a body in order to live in this world! But then, there is this next thing you must believe:

## I am a fallen sinner.

We talked last time about how, when Adam sinned, all people and all creation fell into sin. Let's recite this verse one more time...

**Read Romans 5:12.**

> **¹² Therefore, just as sin came into the world through one man, and death through sin, and so death spread to all men because all sinned—**

Do you know that you are a sinner? I hope you do! Let's read one more verse...

**Read Romans 3:23.**

> **²³ for all have sinned and fall short of the glory of God,**

Are you part of the ALL people this verse is talking about? Yes, you are. So you have been born into this world as a SINNER. That means you are also born spiritually DEAD before God. You are dead in your sins. That doesn't sound too good, does it? It's very bad news.

## I am deserving of hell because of my sin.

**Read Romans 6:23a.**

> **²³ For the wages of sin is death...**

Do you know what WAGES are? **(Allow answers.)** They are what you have to pay for work that is done. So the payment for our sins is what? [Death.] The DEATH spoken of here is spending all eternity in HELL. All people deserve separation from God and life in HELL, because of their sin. Do you know that you deserve HELL too? If you do, you also have to believe this one last bit of bad news...

## I am unable to get to heaven on my own.

Just as your sin deserves hell, it also keeps you out of heaven. Why is that true? **(Allow answers.)** Only those who are without sin can get to heaven. And because you are a sinner by nature, you are not fit for heaven!

But what if you just try really, really hard to be good? Can you become perfectly good? Can you somehow be good enough for heaven? No way!

---

## *Detail your story...*

**Talk to your child about how you thought you were either good enough for heaven or too bad to even have a chance for heaven.**

---

Okay, there is just one more thing about your IDENTITY that you need to believe...

## I am in need of a Savior.

Do you know this is the greatest of all NEEDS? Yes, you need food and water every day. You need oxygen and sleep and a place to live. But your greatest NEED of all is a SAVIOR who can forgive your sin and cleanse all of your unrighteousness. Only then can you escape hell and be fit for heaven. Here's one more verse to hear...

### *Read Luke 19:10.*

### <sup>10</sup> For the Son of Man came to seek and to save the lost.

So, who is this Son of Man who came to save people who are dead in their sins and lost in this world? You probably already know the answer!

*Until we talk again next time...*

# DECLARING THE TRUTH

*Lead your child to continue to profess the faith in his or her words:*

## I believe that I am...

- made in the image of God.
- a human being, body and soul.
- a fallen sinner.
- deserving of hell.
- unable to get to heaven.
- in need of a Savior.

We will add to our profession of the faith, our declaration of the truth, when we talk next time...

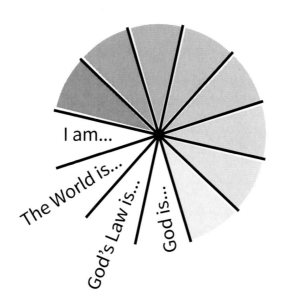

# ESTABLISHED IN THE FAITH
## CONVERSATION: *5*

# Jesus is...

## DIGGING IN

When I say the name JESUS, what is the first thing that comes into your mind? **(Allow answers.)**

JESUS CHRIST is probably the most famous name in human history! So, you may think that everyone knows who Jesus is. And, you may even assume that everyone believes the same things about Jesus. But unfortunately, that's just not true. Not only do many people NOT believe Jesus is real, many more will differ with us on who Jesus is!

## DEFINING TERMS

So, let's begin by simply defining what the terms JESUS and CHRIST really mean. Do you know? **(Allow answers.)**

The name JESUS in English goes all the way back to a Hebrew word that means RESCUE or DELIVER. It can also mean SAVES. When used as a name, it can mean "GOD SAVES." Isn't that interesting?

Then, there's the word CHRIST. That's not Jesus' last name, by the way. It's a name that means ANOINTED ONE or MESSIAH. So Jesus IS the CHRIST, the MESSIAH, anointed by God for a special work and mission.

These two names tell us big things about Jesus, don't they? But we need to learn more about what God's Word says about this very REAL Jesus!

 # DISCUSSING TOGETHER

We ended last time with the BAD NEWS that we are unable to get to heaven on our own. We all need a SAVIOR! So, since JESUS has the very name of "God SAVES," it's time we talk about Him, right? Let's discuss who we believe that...

# Jesus is...

We could say so much about Jesus, couldn't we? What we want to know is what the BIBLE says about Him. And there is so much the Bible says! So let's start with the fact that...

## Jesus is the Son of God.

**Read 2 Corinthians 1:19a.**

¹⁹ **For the Son of God, Jesus Christ, whom we proclaimed among you...**

Jesus is fully God. He is talked about as being the "Second Person" of the Trinity. Remember when we talked about how God is ONE GOD in THREE PERSONS? Well, Jesus is that Second Person. That means Jesus is 100% God, has always and will always be GOD, and is co-equal with the Father and the Holy Spirit. Jesus is God! Here is one more verse about Jesus...

**Read John 1:1.**

¹ **In the beginning was the Word, and the Word was with God, and the Word was God.**

The WORD is Jesus! That leads us to the next point...

## Jesus is the Son of Man.

This was actually one of Jesus' favorite ways of speaking of Himself. Listen to this verse:

**Read Mark 10:45.**

⁴⁵ **For even the Son of Man came not to be served but to serve, and to give his life as a ransom for many.**

Can you tell me the story of Jesus' birth? **(Allow answers.)** As we will talk more about next time, Jesus was born as a baby to Mary, right? We call this the INCARNATION. That's a big word, isn't it? It simply means that God took on FLESH when Jesus was born into this world. Jesus has a body just like you and me!

So, we believe that Jesus is FULLY GOD and FULLY MAN at the same time. He is the only GOD-MAN. Jesus took on flesh and dwelt among His people. But there is much more to say about Jesus...

## Jesus is the Way, the Truth, and the Life.

Listen again to Jesus Himself. **Read John 14:6.**

**⁶ Jesus said to him, "I am the way, and the truth, and the life. No one comes to the Father except through me."**

All through the gospels, Jesus tells us who He is. He is the GOOD SHEPHERD. He is the BREAD OF LIFE. He is the LIGHT OF THE WORLD. He is the RESURRECTION AND THE LIFE. As you just heard, He sums up Himself by saying that He is the only WAY to get to God the Father. He is also the TRUTH and the LIFE. So, what do all these descriptions of Jesus tell you about Him? **(Allow answers.)**

## Jesus is the Mediator.

Here's another important verse. **Read 1 Timothy 2:5.**

**⁵ For there is one God, and there is one mediator between God and men, the man Christ Jesus...**

What is a MEDIATOR? **(Allow answers.)** A mediator is someone who makes peace between two warring enemies.

So, who are the enemies that need to make peace? That's right–you and God! All people are born at war with God. That's why we need Jesus, the mediator! We'll talk more about that later, but we must also believe that...

## Jesus is Lord.

**Read Philippians 2:10-11.**

¹⁰ so that at the name of Jesus every knee should bow, in heaven and on earth and under the earth, ¹¹ and every tongue confess that Jesus Christ is Lord...

---

# Detail your story...

**Tell your child when you first understood Jesus as your LORD and SAVIOR. How old were you? What happened?**

---

Jesus is KING of the universe, right? Another way to say it is that Jesus is LORD. And, as you heard in this verse, one day everyone will know Jesus is LORD and will bow before Him. The question is, will you call Him your LORD now?

## Jesus is Savior.

Remember we said that the name JESUS means "God SAVES." So it should make sense that He is SAVIOR.

Listen to the apostle Paul. **Read Philippians 3:20.**

²⁰ But our citizenship is in heaven, and from it we await a Savior, the Lord Jesus Christ.

In other words, if you are a child of God, you are a citizen of heaven, not of earth. All children of God enjoy the work of the SAVIOR, Jesus Christ. So we will need to talk about this work in the life, death, and resurrection of Jesus in some important conversations yet to come!

But there is one last thing you need to believe about Jesus. The apostle Paul says it so well.

**Read 2 Corinthians 11:4.**

⁴ For if someone comes and proclaims another Jesus than the one we proclaimed, or if you receive a different spirit from the one you received, or if you accept a different gospel from the one you accepted...

What Paul is saying is that there is **no other Jesus.** You must only believe in the Jesus of the Bible. You cannot make up your own image of Jesus. Jesus Christ is who He says He is! So always be careful to know the REAL JESUS, the rest of your life! More about the life of Jesus next time...

#  DECLARING THE TRUTH

*Lead your child to begin to profess the faith in his or her words:*

## I believe that Jesus is...

- the Son of God.
- fully God and Fully Man.
- the Way, the Truth, and the Life.
- the Mediator.
- the Lord and King of the Universe.
- the Savior of the World.

We will add to our profession of the faith, our declaration of the truth, when we talk again next time…

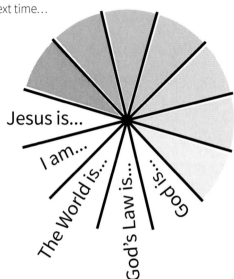

# ESTABLISHED IN THE FAITH
## CONVERSATION: *6*

# Jesus lived...

 ## DIGGING IN

What's the difference between a REAL person and an IMAGINARY one? **(Allow answers.)** These are two opposites, aren't they? One really lived, the other is "made up" fantasy. So who is one of your favorite imaginary people? **(Allow answers.)**

Unfortunately, there are people who think Jesus Christ is just imaginary—made up by His followers. Is that true? No way! Jesus Christ really lived, and still lives today!

 ## DEFINING TERMS

We used an important word that I want to review with you: INCARNATION. Do you remember what it means? **(Allow answers.)** To become INCARNATE is to take on human flesh. It is to have a body. Does God have a body like people do? No! But God the Son does! Jesus took on human flesh and lived among us.

Why is this important to know about Jesus? Because it means that Jesus is not imaginary, or a ghost, or some make-believe superhero. He is the Son of God, who came into the flesh as "God with us."

So, even now, Jesus has a glorified body as the living Son of God. We will talk more about that in our next conversation. Today, let's think about the amazing life of Christ.

# DISCUSSING TOGETHER

Where do we learn about the life of Jesus? **(Allow answers.)** Yes, we read about His life on earth in the GOSPELS–the first four books of the New Testament. As we read those amazing accounts, we learn all about how…

# Jesus lived...

If you claim to be a follower of Jesus, then it makes sense that you need to know how Jesus lived, right? How can you follow someone you don't know anything about? So let's briefly review the life of Jesus.

### Jesus lived a human life.

Did Jesus eat and drink? Yes. Did Jesus sleep? Yes. Did Jesus walk and talk and work? Yes! In other words, Jesus Christ, the Son of God, lived just like you and I do. He grew up from a baby, to a child, to a youth, to an adult. He had family and friends. He lived for over thirty years on the same earth that we live on today. Isn't that amazing? But Jesus wasn't just another human, was He?

### Jesus was tempted, but never sinned.

Do you remember when Satan first tempted Jesus? Can you tell me what happened? **(Allow answers.)** Three different times, the devil tempted Jesus in the wilderness. And these were very hard temptations! So did Jesus sin? No!

Listen to this verse. **Read Hebrews 4:15.**

> **15 For we do not have a high priest who is unable to sympathize with our weaknesses, but one who in every respect has been tempted as we are, yet without sin.**

This is speaking of Jesus. So did Jesus EVER sin? No! You and I sin every day, but Jesus never sinned. He perfectly obeyed in every way.

### Jesus submitted to the will of His Father.

How did Jesus know what to do while He lived on earth? Did He just do whatever He wanted, or what people wanted Him to do? No way!

Listen to Jesus' own words. **Read John 6:38.**

**38 For I have come down from heaven, not to do my own will but the will of him who sent me.**

Who sent Jesus to live on earth? That's right, God the Father did. Jesus' entire life was committed to carrying out the perfect will of God.

## Jesus proclaimed the gospel of the Kingdom of God.

As you read through the four gospels, you will see that Jesus is often preaching and teaching. He is regularly called TEACHER by those who listen to Him. But what does Jesus spend His time proclaiming?

Listen to Mark 1. **Read Mark 1:14-15.**

**14 Now after John was arrested, Jesus came into Galilee, proclaiming the gospel of God, 15 and saying, "The time is fulfilled, and the kingdom of God is at hand; repent and believe in the gospel."**

Jesus spent His time on earth proclaiming the good news of salvation! He taught people all about the kingdom of God since He is the KING!

Have you heard any of Jesus' parables that He taught? Can you tell me one? **(Allow answers.)** Most of these parables teach us about life in God's Kingdom. Jesus lived in such a way to proclaim the good news of the Kingdom of God!

## Jesus powerfully pointed to God.

Did Jesus do incredibly amazing miracles? Of course He did! Can you tell me any? **(Allow answers.)** But why did He do things like feed five thousand men with five loaves and two fish, or calm the sea? **(Allow answers.)**

Listen to Jesus again. **Read John 10:38.**

**38 but if I do them, even though you do not believe me, believe the works, that you may know and understand that the Father is in me and I am in the Father.**

Jesus did lots of powerful miracles to show people the Father and the way to the Father!

CONVERSATION *6* (Jesus lived...)

Some of Jesus' greatest miracles were healing those with diseases and casting out demons. Have you heard some of those stories? So why did Jesus spend some of His time healing people--instead of just preaching to them?

Listen. **Read Matthew 9:36.**

**³⁶ When he saw the crowds, he had compassion for them, because they were harassed and helpless, like sheep without a shepherd.**

---

## Detail your story...

**Talk to your child about how Jesus has worked powerfully in your life and how you have seen His compassion on display.**

---

Jesus is the GREAT SHEPHERD, right? And so His life on earth was dedicated to caring for His people. He had great compassion on them, as He does for you and me today. Now, that's good news!

### *Jesus lived a perfectly righteous life.*

That's the most important thing to know about the life of Jesus! If He did not live a perfectly holy and righteous life, then He could not be our Savior. He would just be another sinner in need of a Savior.

Listen. **Read 1 John 2:1b.**

**¹ But if anyone does sin, we have an advocate with the Father, Jesus Christ the righteous.**

Only because of the sinless perfection of Jesus do we have a way to the Father. But there's more to this good news about Jesus, isn't there? We will talk about the perfect DEATH of Jesus next time!

# DECLARING THE TRUTH

*Lead your child to continue to profess the faith in his or her words:*

## I believe that Jesus lived...

- a perfectly righteous human life.
- a life tempted, without sin.
- in submission to the Father.
- to proclaim the gospel of the Kingdom
- to powerfully point to the Father.
- to compassionately care for people.

We will add to our profession of the faith, our declaration of the truth, when we talk next time...

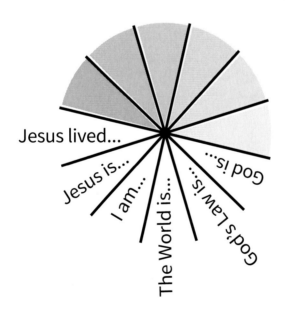

# ESTABLISHED IN THE FAITH
## CONVERSATION: 7

# Jesus died...

 ## DIGGING IN

Wouldn't it have been great if you and I were alive when Jesus walked on the earth? Maybe we could have been in Bethlehem when He was born, or witnessed Him walking on the water, or even have had a sickness healed by Jesus! If you could have witnessed one event, what would it be? **(Allow answers.)**

Have you thought that the greatest event of Jesus' life was actually His DEATH?

 ## DEFINING TERMS

As we talk today about the death of Jesus, we need to define a couple of very important terms. The first is CRUCIFIXION. Crucifixion is the killing of a criminal by nailing him to a wooden cross. It is an extremely painful way to die. The Roman empire used CRUCIFIXION to execute people.

A second important term is RESURRECTION. What does that word mean? **(Allow answers.)** Yes, RESURRECTION is the coming back to life of a dead person. Is that something that happens every day? No way! When someone dies, he or she usually stays dead!

Here's one more important term for today: ATONEMENT. Atonement refers to the covering over and forgiving of our sins because of the death and resurrection of Jesus Christ. That's a very important word, isn't it? The crucifixion and resurrection enable the atonement!

 DISCUSSING TOGETHER

We have spent time talking about who Jesus is and how Jesus lived on this earth. As we continue to profess our faith in this Jesus together, it is essential to think about why...

# *Jesus died...*

The Bible clearly tells us HOW Jesus died. At the end of every gospel, we can read the events that led up to His arrest, His false condemnation, and His death on the cross between two criminals. Many people believe that Jesus died this way. But not everyone believes in WHY He had to die this way and what it accomplished. So let's talk about it!

## *Jesus died as a sinless, innocent man.*

Crucifixion was the execution of a guilty criminal for his sins. So, does this mean that since Jesus was crucified, that He was guilty of sin? No way!

Listen to I Peter 3:18. **Read 1 Peter 3:18.**

**¹⁸ For Christ also suffered once for sins, the righteous for the unrighteous, that he might bring us to God, being put to death in the flesh but made alive in the spirit...**

Do you hear it? Jesus died ONCE for sins, as the RIGHTEOUS for the unrighteous. Who are the unrighteous? You and me! Jesus did not deserve to die on the cross. He was totally innocent as the perfect Son of God.

## *Jesus died out of obedience to the will of God.*

Before Jesus went to the cross, He spent an intense time of prayer to His Father. Do you remember what He prayed? Understanding what bearing the weight of the sins of His people meant, he prayed these words...

**Read Luke 22:42.**

**⁴² Father, if you are willing, remove this cup from me. Nevertheless, not my will, but yours, be done.**

As He did in His life, Jesus obeyed the Father in His death.

## Jesus died because sin has to be punished.

Remember this verse? **Read Romans 6:23.**

²³ For the wages of sin is death, but the free gift of God is eternal life in Christ Jesus our Lord.

We already know that sin must be punished, and that punishment is DEATH. Someone has to pay the wages of sin, right? If Jesus doesn't die on the cross then ALL sinners must die and go to hell forever.

## Jesus died to satisfy God's wrath.

God's wrath is His holy, just, and righteous anger. So, what makes God angry?

Listen to Romans 1. **Read Romans 1:18.**

¹⁸ For the wrath of God is revealed from heaven against all ungodliness and unrighteousness of men, who by their unrighteousness suppress the truth.

Do you hear it? God is angry at all of our ungodliness and unrighteousness. In other words, God is angry at our SIN all the time. His holy wrath must be satisfied!

Which leads us to this verse. **Read 1 John 2:2.**

² He is the propitiation for our sins, and not for ours only but also for the sins of the whole world.

Say that big word with me: PROPITIATION. It means that Jesus' death on the cross satisfies the anger of God for the sins of His people. What great news, right?

## Jesus died for the forgiveness of sin.

We already know that we need our sins forgiven, right? Well, that is why Jesus died!

**Read Ephesians 1:7.**

⁷ In him we have redemption through his blood, the forgiveness of our trespasses, according to the riches of his grace.

# Detail your story...

**Tell your child a personal story of needing the blood of Christ to cover your sins. Share how great the atonement really is!**

The death of Jesus on the cross is the grace of God for our sin. We can only be forgiven of our sins because Jesus makes ATONEMENT for our sins. His blood covers all of our sin, now and forever!

## Jesus died to give His people eternal life.

We need this verse one more time. **Read John 3:16.**

¹⁶ **For God so loved the world, that he gave his only Son, that whoever believes in him should not perish but have eternal life.**

I hope you know it by heart! It sums up why Jesus needed to die on the cross. All people are dead in their sin, with no hope of life. The only way to have eternal life is in the death of Jesus Christ.

As we read in 1 Peter 2. **Read 1 Peter 2:24.**

²⁴ **He himself bore our sins in his body on the tree, that we might die to sin and live to righteousness. By his wounds you have been healed.**

## Jesus died to conquer death.

But we must end by confessing that Jesus didn't just die on the cross for our sins. God raised Him from the dead!

Listen to Jesus' words. **Read John 11:25-26.**

²⁵ **Jesus said to her, "I am the resurrection and the life. Whoever believes in me, though he die, yet shall he live,** ²⁶ **and everyone who lives and believes in me shall never die. Do you believe this?"**

That's Jesus' question to you too! Do you believe that Jesus died and rose again for your sins? Do you believe He died to conquer death so you never have to die and go to hell for your sins? We'll continue talking next time...

 # DECLARING THE TRUTH

## *Lead your child to begin to profess the faith in his or her words:*

### I believe that Jesus died...

- as a sinless, innocent Man.
- out of obedience to the will of God.
- because sin has to be punished.
- to satisfy God's wrath.
- for the forgiveness of sin and eternal life for His people.
- to gain the victory over death and hell.

We will add to our profession of the faith, our declaration of the truth, when we talk again next time...

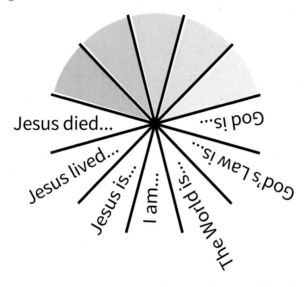

# ESTABLISHED IN THE FAITH
## CONVERSATION: *8*

# My life is...

## DIGGING IN

If I asked you to describe your LIFE right now, what would you say? I would hope you would tell me how GREAT it is, how wonderful your family is, and how hopeful you are for the future!

So, go ahead: What is your LIFE like right now? **(Allow answers.)** Do you think that every person in the world would describe his or her life the same way? What about all other Christians? Hopefully, there are some similarities!

## DEFINING TERMS

As we dive into another conversation about our faith in Jesus, let's define another important term: UNION. Do you know what that word means? **(Allow answers.)**

Marriage is a UNION between one man and one woman, as husband and wife. According to God's Word, two people become ONE flesh. So, a UNION in this usage is a deep, connected relationship between two people.

When a person becomes a Christian, he or she experiences a UNION as well. To whom do we become UNITED? **(Allow answers.)**That's right, the person becomes UNITED with Jesus Christ! Christianity is a relationship between Jesus and His people! So, as we'll discuss further in a moment, UNION with Christ defines our relationship with Jesus.

# DISCUSSING TOGETHER

So, if we know what we believe about Jesus–who He is, how He lived, and how He died and lives again, how does that connect to your life? In other words, when I put my faith in Jesus alone for my salvation, I need to be able to talk about what...

# *My life is...*

Do you think your life is the SAME as it was before you put your faith in Jesus? Before you came to rest in Him alone for your salvation? No way! First of all, you must know that...

## *My life is not my own.*

Listen to the apostle Paul. **Read 1 Corinthians 6:19-20.**

> **¹⁹ Or do you not know that your body is a temple of the Holy Spirit within you, whom you have from God? You are not your own, ²⁰ for you were bought with a price. So glorify God in your body.**

All through the New Testament, language is used of "buying" when describing our relationship with Christ. In those days, a slave was "bought" in order to be freed from slavery. What are all people "slaves" to? Sin and death! So, in order to be freed from sin, Jesus "buys" us with the cost of His own blood. And if Jesus has bought you, you are not your own! Your life is the Lord's!

## *My life is "In Christ."*

Here's another important verse. **Read Galatians 2:20.**

> **²⁰ I have been crucified with Christ. It is no longer I who live, but Christ who lives in me. And the life I now live in the flesh I live by faith in the Son of God, who loved me and gave himself for me.**

Remember how we defined the term UNION? This is what I was talking about! When you become a Christian, your life is "In Christ" and Christ "lives in" you! Is that hard to understand? It should be, because it is a great mystery. But it is also true. Christians live because Christ lives in them. He alone is the resurrection and the LIFE! We can only put sin to death because Christ, our life, lives in us. That leads us to another very important truth...

## My life is filled with God's grace.

What does the word GRACE mean? **(Allow answers.)** Grace is God's unmerited favor to sinners. Can you earn God's GRACE? No way! It is the free gift from God.

Listen to this verse. **Read 2 Corinthians 12:9.**

> ⁹ **But he said to me, "My grace is sufficient for you, for my power is made perfect in weakness." Therefore I will boast all the more gladly of my weaknesses, so that the power of Christ may rest upon me.**

We need God's grace for salvation AND for living out the Christian life. Do you ever feel weak? You will! And you will need to learn how to live in the strength of Christ instead of your own strength. His grace is sufficient for you to live this difficult life until Christ returns.

## My life is hidden in and protected by Christ.

Here's another great text. **Read Colossians 3:1-3.**

> ¹ **If then you have been raised with Christ, seek the things that are above, where Christ is, seated at the right hand of God. ² Set your minds on things that are above, not on things that are on earth. ³ For you have died, and your life is hidden with Christ in God.**

Have you ever hidden in a closet because some big storm or tornado was coming? Sometimes it's a good thing to hide, especially when danger is close by. Well, we have the best hiding place in the world–Jesus! Our lives are hidden in Him, so we are protected by Him. We have nothing to fear in our lives because of our faithful and strong Savior.

Now, does that mean when I become a Christian, I will never suffer again? No way! We still live in a fallen world. The Christian will suffer from attacks by Satan, his own sin, other people, and from life in general. But because we have "died" with Christ, our future is secure. Our lives are safe and secure in Christ!

## *My life is made for good works.*

Listen to the apostle Paul again. **Read Ephesians 2:8-10.**

> [8] For by grace you have been saved through faith. And this is not your own doing; it is the gift of God, [9] not a result of works, so that no one may boast. [10] For we are his workmanship, created in Christ Jesus for good works, which God prepared beforehand, that we should walk in them.

We have talked about some of these truths already. So focus on verse 10–we are His workmanship, created in Christ Jesus for WHAT? Good works! What are good works? **(Allow answers.)** Good works are the good things we do out of obedience and faith, for the glory of God. Good works are connected to a true and living faith. In another passage, James says: "Faith without works is dead." So the life of the Christian is to be filled with the doing of good things for God and other people. We can only do good works by the grace of God!

---

# *Detail your story...*

**Talk to your child about how you are living out your faith in Jesus Christ. What are some good works that God is doing through you?**

---

## *My life is a new creation.*

The last and best thing about the Christian life is that the old becomes new!

Listen. **Read 2 Corinthians 5:17.**

> [17] Therefore, if anyone is in Christ, he is a new creation. The old has passed away; behold, the new has come.

Sin just makes everything old, worn out, and rotten. A life without Christ is just a life of death. But when you put your faith in Jesus, He makes you a NEW creation. Everything about you is made new–your heart, your mind, your soul, your strength–all renewed in the image of Christ. That means you will be able to walk in the newness of Christ! You will learn more and more to be like Jesus!

# DECLARING THE TRUTH

*Lead your child to continue to profess the faith in his or her words:*

## I believe that my life is...

- not my own.
- "in Christ."
- filled with God's grace.
- hidden in and protected by Christ.
- made for good works.
- a new creation.

We will add to our profession of the faith, our declaration of the truth, when we talk next time...

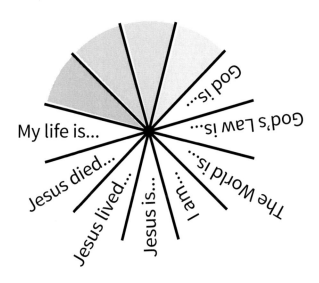

ESTABLISHED IN THE FAITH

# CONVERSATION: 9

# The Holy Spirit is...

 DIGGING IN

What does a car need in order to run? [Gas.] What does a flashlight need in order to shine? [Batteries.] What does a television need in order to work? [Electricity.] So what do all these things have in common? **(Allow answers.)** Yes, they all need a POWER source to make them work!

We will have a conversation today about the POWER needed for God's people to do their "work" and to please God.

 DEFINING TERMS

In our very first conversation, we used the term TRINITY to describe God. What do we mean when we say we believe in the TRINITY? **(Allow answers.)** Yes, we believe that our ONE God exists in THREE persons–the Father, the Son, and the Holy Spirit.

So today we are going to talk about the THIRD PERSON of the Trinity, the Holy Spirit. He is co-equal with the Father and the Son. He co-exsists with the Father and the Son. The Holy Spirit is God!

Here's what I want you to always believe: There is no true Christian faith without belief in the TRINITY! When you put your faith in Jesus Christ, you acknowledge that He is God, the Father is God, and the Holy Spirit is God. All three members of the TRINITY are active in your salvation and in your life!

 DISCUSSING TOGETHER

So if we believe in God, and we believe in Jesus, then we also believe in the Holy Spirit. But what makes the Holy Spirit unique and special? How does He work in our lives as Christians? That's what we need to talk about–truths about who...

# *The Holy Spirit is...*

If Jesus is sitting on the right hand of the Father in heaven, where is the Holy Spirit?

## *The Holy Spirit is dwelling in God's people.*

Listen. **Read John 14:17.**

**¹⁷ even the Spirit of truth, whom the world cannot receive, because it neither sees him nor knows him. You know him, for he dwells with you and will be in you.**

The Holy Spirit, also known as the "Spirit of truth," lives with the Christian and IN the Christian!

Listen to one more verse. **Read 1 Corinthians 3:16.**

**¹⁶ Do you not know that you are God's temple and that God's Spirit dwells in you?**

Wow! What an amazing truth! When you put your faith in Jesus Christ as your Savior and Lord, the Holy Spirit comes and lives within you. Why is it so important that you have the Holy Spirit in you? **(Allow answers.)**

The Holy Spirit is the Giver of Life.

All people may look like they have LIFE in them, but the only ones who have true LIFE are Christians. Listen to what Jesus said about the Holy Spirit...

**Read John 6:63.**

**⁶³ It is the Spirit who gives life; the flesh is no help at all. The words that I have spoken to you are spirit and life.**

So Jesus gives us life by His WORD and through the Holy Spirit. Without a life-giving Spirit, we have only our own flesh to depend on. Is that enough to live this life? No way!

## *The Holy Spirit is our Helper and Comforter.*

Listen to Jesus again. **Read John 14:26.**

**26 But the Helper, the Holy Spirit, whom the Father will send in my name, he will teach you all things and bring to your remembrance all that I have said to you.**

What sort of HELP do you and I need to live this life for Jesus Christ? **(Allow answers.)** According to Jesus, we need the Holy Spirit to TEACH us God's Word and REMIND us of all that Jesus has said. So the Holy Spirit is our greatest TEACHER and COUNSELOR, isn't He?

The name HELPER used to describe the Holy Spirit can also be translated COMFORTER. One of the best ways the Holy Spirit helps us in our weakness is by COMFORTING us. Can you think of times where you have needed the Spirit of COMFORT? I can!

## *The Holy Spirit is the Spirit of Power.*

Do you remember how we began this conversation? Just as machines need a power source, so do people! And there is only one place for us to get power to live, right? The Holy Spirit gives us the power of God in our lives.

Listen. **Read Romans 15:13.**

**13 May the God of hope fill you with all joy and peace in believing, so that by the power of the Holy Spirit you may abound in hope.**

The Holy Spirit gives us power to have joy, peace, and hope in this difficult life. But He also gives us power for other things too.

**Read Acts 1:8.**

**8 But you will receive power when the Holy Spirit has come upon you, and you will be my witnesses in Jerusalem and in all Judea and Samaria, and to the end of the earth."**

These words were spoken to the apostles as the Spirit gave them power to be His witnesses. But all Christians need the power of the Spirit to witness for Jesus too, right? The Holy Spirit gives us power when we are at our weakest!

## *The Holy Spirit is our Leader.*

Now listen to this verse. **Read Romans 8:14.**

¹⁴ For all who are led by the Spirit of God are sons of God.

And this one. **Read Galatians 5:16.**

¹⁶ But I say, walk by the Spirit, and you will not gratify the desires of the flesh.

Do you ever play the game, "Follow the Leader"? Well, that describes what living the Christian life is all about. It is a life of FOLLOWING the Spirit's lead. It is compared to "walking in step" with the Spirit. Do you know how easy it is for all of us to do things our own way, or follow all the wrong people? The Christian life is marked by knowing the Spirit is our LEADER, and by God's grace, following His lead rather than our own.

## *Detail your story...*

**Tell your child your own story of following the Spirit's lead. You may even want to relate how you have resisted His leadership at times!**

## *The Holy Spirit is interceding for us.*

Listen to this good news. **Read Romans 8:26-27.**

²⁶ Likewise the Spirit helps us in our weakness. For we do not know what to pray for as we ought, but the Spirit himself intercedes for us with groanings too deep for words. ²⁷ And he who searches hearts knows what is the mind of the Spirit, because the Spirit intercedes for the saints according to the will of God.

What does it mean that the Holy Spirit INTERCEDES for us? **(Allow answers.)** Yes, it means He is PRAYING for us! Why do we need the Spirit to pray for us? Because we are weak. Because we are sinful. Because the Spirit knows the will of God for us! Thank God for His Holy Spirit!

# DECLARING THE TRUTH

*Lead your child to begin to profess the faith in his or her words:*

## I believe that the Holy Spirit is...

- dwelling in His people.
- the Giver of life.
- our Helper and Comforter.
- our Power to live.
- our Leader.
- interceding for us.

We will add to our profession of the faith, our declaration of the truth, when we talk again next time...

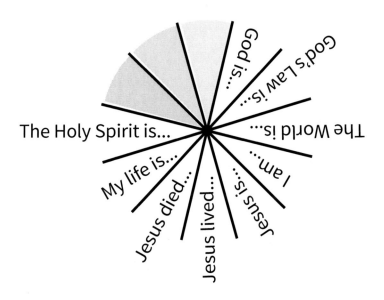

# ESTABLISHED IN THE FAITH

## CONVERSATION: *10*

# The Church is...

## DIGGING IN

Here's a question for you: What words would you use to describe our CHURCH? Friendly? Boring? Exciting? Family? **(Allow answers.)** Has CHURCH become important to you?

Think about this question: Can you live your whole life as a Christian and not be a part of a local church? That's a tough one, isn't it? Some people think of the church as optional, while others see it as central to their lives. But what does the Bible say, so we believe the truth about the CHURCH?

## DEFINING TERMS

Let's talk about the word CHURCH for a moment. Is the CHURCH the building where we go to worship? Yes and no. Most CHURCHES have various buildings for people to gather to worship God. But that isn't really THE CHURCH.

To understand better, let's learn the Greek word for CHURCH. It is EKKLESIA. This word literally means "assembly" or "congregation." So a CHURCH is really the PEOPLE who gather together as a local congregation.

So, we don't GO to CHURCH, we ARE part of the CHURCH. Christians all over the world assemble in local congregations in order to worship the One True God. CHURCH is not an event; it is the corporate group of believers who are following Jesus together. This will be the focus of our conversation today!

# DISCUSSING TOGETHER

There are all sorts of ideas about what a CHURCH should "look like" and what it should be all about. But it is most important to know what the Bible teaches us about the CHURCH, right? Christians are called to be the CHURCH, so we must know what...

# *The Church is...*

Let's start with the most important truth we must believe, or we will never understand the CHURCH.

### *The church is led by Christ, her Head.*

What would you say if I asked you, "Who's in charge of your church? **(Allow answers.)** You may be tempted to say it's your pastor, or your elders, or some other human being. Even though God has appointed people to lead the local church, they are not ultimately in charge. Jesus is the head of the church!

Listen to this verse. **Read Colossians 1:18.**

> **18 And he is the head of the body, the church. He is the beginning, the firstborn from the dead, that in everything he might be preeminent.**

Whom is Paul talking about? Jesus! Jesus is the head of the CHURCH. The CHURCH is HIS!

Here's another verse to know. **Read Ephesians 5:23.**

> **23 For the husband is the head of the wife even as Christ is the head of the church, his body, and is himself its Savior.**

This is why we can also say that the CHURCH is the BRIDE of Christ. As a husband is spiritual head over his wife, so is Jesus the HEAD of His CHURCH!

### *The Church of Jesus Christ is visible.*

This makes sense, doesn't it? When people gather together to worship God, it is SEEN by the world. It is the visible, worshiping community. What things does a VISIBLE CHURCH do? **(Allow answers.)** The visible church witnesses, teaches, sings, serves, has fellowship with one another, participates in the sacraments, etc.

So people all over the world JOIN local churches and become part of the VISIBLE church. There are differences of how a person becomes a MEMBER of a local church, but, generally speaking, people make a public profession of faith in Jesus in order to declare their membership in the visible church. **(Share how your church receives its members.)**

But are all people who are members of a visible church automatically Christians? Not necessarily! Jesus told several parables that teach us how the church is made up of wheat or sheep (true Christians, followers of Christ), and weeds of wolves (false members, false followers of Christ); sheep, and wolves. That leads us to our next truth...

## The Church of Jesus Christ is invisible.

That sounds sort of funny, doesn't it? What do we mean? Let's start with this: All of God's elect, chosen people of ALL time in ALL places make up the invisible church. When you truly put your faith in Jesus Christ as your Savior and Lord, you too become part of the invisible church! We call it INVISIBLE because only God knows the number of the elect–who are really Christians and who are not.

So, the invisible church is the true, universal people of God. It includes all who are "in Christ." Therefore, when a visible church is meeting, are ALL members automatically part of the invisible church? No! Only God knows our hearts. Yet, all members of the invisible church are called and commanded to gather as the visible church in this world.

## The Church of Jesus Christ is a family.

Listen to these verses. **Read Ephesians 2:19-20.**

**[19] So then you are no longer strangers and aliens, but you are fellow citizens with the saints and members of the household of God, [20] built on the foundation of the apostles and prophets, Christ Jesus himself being the cornerstone...**

Do you hear it? When you become a Christian, you join the household of

God! As we have talked about already, you are ADOPTED as a child of God, with Jesus as your older brother. So the CHURCH is to operate as a FAMILY—brothers and sisters living together in a loving community. Does that describe our church?

## The Church is the Body of Christ.

Listen. **Read Romans 12:4-5.**

**4 For as in one body we have many members, and the members do not all have the same function, 5 so we, though many, are one body in Christ, and individually members one of another.**

All throughout Paul's letters, the CHURCH is compared to your human body. Just as the body has many members, the CHURCH (as the body of Christ) must work together in submission to Christ. So God has given all of us different gifts and talents that we use to serve one another and to reach the world for Jesus! Christians all connect to each other as the CHURCH because we need each other.

---

## *Detail your story...*

**Talk to your child about how you have served in your local church in the past, and what you are doing in the present.**

---

## The Church is the community of faith in Christ.

So does it makes sense to have Christians who are not a part of a local, visible church? That would be like you not living in our home, ever coming to a family meal, or participating in any family event. Or, it would be like you are a hand that thinks he can live without an arm, or a brain, or a skeleton. Or, it is like living in a community, but never knowing anyone or doing anything in your community.

The Church is the family of God, the body of Christ, and the community of faith. We are called to be connected to one another, under our head, Jesus

Christ. Unfortunately, it is easy to be disconnected, uninvolved, and self-centered. As you profess your faith in Jesus, I pray you will also profess your love for HIS CHURCH!

 # DECLARING THE TRUTH

*Lead your child to continue to profess the faith in his or her words:*

## I believe that the Church is...

- under the Lordship of Christ, her head.
- both visible and invisible.
- the Family of God.
- the Body of Christ.
- the Community of faith in Christ.

We will add to our profession of the faith, our declaration of the truth, when we talk next time...

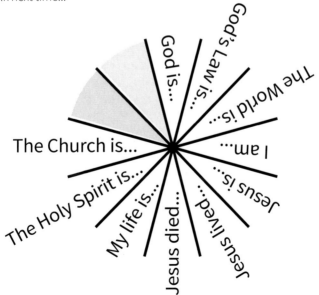

# ESTABLISHED IN THE FAITH
## CONVERSATION: 11

# The Lord's Supper is...

## DIGGING IN

What's your favorite meal of the day? **(Allow answers.)** And what's your favorite food to eat at that meal? **(Allow answers.)**

Sometimes, it's the food that makes a meal great. But at other times, it's the people you are eating it with that make it so special–like a birthday dinner, or Thanksgiving dinner. Think about how meals are meant to be RELATIONAL, and we'll talk about it in a minute.

## DEFINING TERMS

Here's another important word you need to know: SACRAMENT. Have you heard it before?

A SACRAMENT is a holy sign and seal of the covenant of grace. God gave SACRAMENTS to His people as visible picture of the work of Jesus Christ in our hearts. They are also seals of the promises of God in our lives. Those who receive the SACRAMENTS are set apart from the world and dedicated to Jesus.

The Bible teaches that God instituted TWO SACRAMENTS. Do you know what they are? **(Allow answers.)** The two sacraments are BAPTISM and the LORD'S SUPPER. You may have already been baptized. That SACRA-MENT is applied once. But the LORD'S SUPPER is meant to be received over and over again. So our focus today will be on learning more about the LORD'S SUPPER.

# DISCUSSING TOGETHER

When you make a profession of faith in Jesus Christ and become a communing member of a local church, you have new privileges and responsibilities. One of the greatest privileges is that you now get to enjoy the LORD'S SUPPER. So that means it's very important that you learn what...

# The Lord's Supper is...

Let's begin with this truth:

### The Lord's Supper was instituted by Christ.

Do you remember that our Lord Jesus celebrated the Passover with His disciples right before He was betrayed, arrested, and crucified? We call this Passover meal Jesus' LAST SUPPER.

But this LAST SUPPER is significant for another reason. Jesus transformed the Jewish Passover meal into what we now call the LORD'S SUPPER. Have you seen us celebrate the LORD'S SUPPER in church? Jesus instituted this SUPPER and gave us new PICTURES (signs) to teach us about Himself and what He does for us. That leads us to our next truth...

### The Lord's Supper is eating bread and drinking juice.

Why do we eat bread at the Lord's Supper? Listen to what Jesus said. **Read Luke 22:19.**

**¹⁹ And he took bread, and when he had given thanks, he broke it and gave it to them, saying, "This is my body, which is given for you. Do this in remembrance of me."**

Do you hear it? The bread represents the physical, incarnated body of Christ which was broken for us on the cross.

And what about the juice that we drink?

Listen to Jesus again. **Read Luke 22:20.**

**²⁰ And likewise the cup after they had eaten, saying, "This cup that is poured out for you is the new covenant in my blood."**

So the cup of juice is a sign that points to the BLOOD of Christ shed for us. It is the new COVENANT of God's forgiveness in Christ!

## The Lord's Supper proclaims the death of Christ.

Listen to the apostle Paul. **Read 1 Corinthians 11:26.**

**26 For as often as you eat this bread and drink the cup, you proclaim the Lord's death until he comes.**

So every time you take the Lord's Supper, you are proclaiming to yourself and to the world that Christ died for sinners! Only by the breaking of Jesus' body and the shedding of His blood do we enjoy forgiveness of our sins.

## The Lord's Supper is communion.

You may hear your pastor use the word COMMUNION when talking about the Lord's Supper. Communion and the Lord's Supper are the same thing. Calling it COMMUNION reminds us that we are COMMUNING with God and with His people. In other words, it is the COMMUNITY of believers that comes together to share in this sacrament. As we have already talked about, when you are connected to Christ, you are also connected to His body of believers, the CHURCH!

## The Lord's Supper is to be celebrated regularly.

Think about if you decided to only eat and drink every once in a while. Would that sustain you physically? No way! Just like we need a regular meal for our bodies, we need the LORD'S SUPPER to sustain us spiritually. It is what we call "a means of grace" for the Christian life. So you will see that your church celebrates the LORD'S SUPPER regularly to always remind us of Jesus!

## The Lord's Supper must be celebrated properly.

Listen to these verses. **Read 1 Corinthians 11:27-28.**

**27 Whoever, therefore, eats the bread or drinks the cup of the Lord in an unworthy manner will be guilty concerning the body and blood of the Lord. 28 Let a person examine himself, then, and so eat of the bread and drink of the cup.**

Is anyone WORTHY to take the Lord's Supper? No way! We are all sinners in need of the grace of God. Paul is NOT saying that we must be perfect in order to receive communion.

But we are to eat and drink in a worthy MANNER. Verse 28 helps us understand what this worthy manner is. We are to EXAMINE ourselves with these questions: (1) Am I a Christian? (2) Do I know I'm a sinner? (3) Do I know that I need Jesus? (4) Are there sins I need to confess and change? Do you see how this is a WORTHY manner to receive the Lord's Supper? We are to come humbly to Christ, enjoying His grace for our lives!

---

## *Detail your story...*

**Tell your child about your experience taking the Lord's Supper, as well as any other specific instruction on the sacrament itself.**

---

## *The Lord's Supper is a spiritual supper.*

There are some who believe that Jesus Christ is physically present in the bread and juice. When Jesus said, "This is my body," they believe the bread actually becomes His body!

But this is not true. Jesus is not physically present in the bread or juice. He is sitting at the right hand of God the Father in heaven!

Listen to this last verse. **Read 1 Corinthians 10:16.**

**16 The cup of blessing that we bless, is it not a participation in the blood of Christ? The bread that we break, is it not a participation in the body of Christ?**

So Christ is present in the Lord's Supper—but only SPIRITUALLY. This is a spiritual supper, and we commune with Christ spiritually. Isn't that good news? Jesus Christ communes with us in this amazing sacrament. He feeds us spiritually, and points our hearts and minds to His presence in our lives!

# DECLARING THE TRUTH

*Lead your child to continue to profess the faith in his or her words:*

*I believe that the Lord's Supper is...*

- instituted by Christ.
- proclaiming the death of Christ.
- communion with God and one another.
- to be celebrated regularly and properly.
- a spiritual supper.

We will add to our profession of the faith, our declaration of the truth, when we talk again next time...

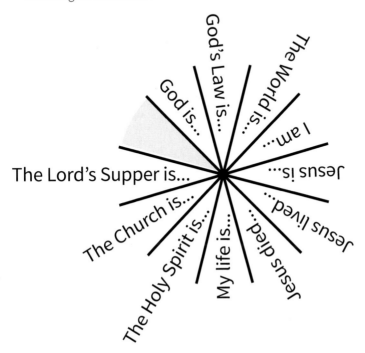

# ESTABLISHED IN THE FAITH
## CONVERSATION: *12*

# The Future is...

 ## DIGGING IN

We have arrived at our last conversation about the Christian faith. Does that mean we will never talk about Jesus again, or about what He is doing in our lives, or what we truly believe as Christians? No way! This is just the beginning of a lifelong conversation.

So if I asked you what your life will be like in thirty years from now, what would you say? **(Allow answers.)** The best answer is: Only God knows!

 ## DEFINING TERMS

Here's a great big word for you: ESCHATOLOGY. What in the world does that mean? Well, the simple definition of ESCHATOLOGY is: "The study of the future, or the study of last things."

As we just said, only God knows the future. So why do we even have to talk about the future? Well, for one thing, we need to learn what God's Word says about "last things." Believe it or not, having a biblical ESCHATOLOGY will help you live well in the present!

As you grow up, you will think a lot about the future and things to come. You may even get anxious from time to time. All of us speculate about what the future holds. Thankfully, Christians know WHO holds our future!

# DISCUSSING TOGETHER

Does believing in Jesus make a difference in the way you look at the FUTURE? Yes, it does! Being established in your faith in Jesus Christ impacts everything you do and every day you live on this earth. So, let's talk about what Christians believe...

# *The Future is...*

This is the most important truth to believe:

### *The future is in God's hands.*

If that is true, who does NOT hold your future? **(Allow answers.)** You don't! I don't! Other people don't! That's great news, isn't it?

Listen to these verses. **Read James 4:13-15.**

> **¹³ Come now, you who say, "Today or tomorrow we will go into such and such a town and spend a year there and trade and make a profit"— ¹⁴ yet you do not know what tomorrow will bring. What is your life? For you are a mist that appears for a little time and then vanishes. ¹⁵ Instead you ought to say, "If the Lord wills, we will live and do this or that."**

There is nothing wrong with making plans for the future. The Christian makes plans with the view that God is in charge of the future. We are able to do "this or that" because God is in control!

### *The future is about my sanctification.*

We talked about this big word before–SANCTIFICATION. Do you remember what it means? **(Allow answers.)** This is the process of being made more and more like Jesus each and every day! As a Christian, you will be dying more to your sin and living more to Jesus.

Listen to this verse. **Read Romans 6:22.**

> **²² But now that you have been set free from sin and have become slaves of God, the fruit you get leads to sanctification and its end, eternal life.**

Do you hear what's in store for your future? Sanctification every day and then, in the end, eternal life. How does it change your thinking about your life if you know it is all about your SANCTIFICATION? **(Allow answers.)**

### The future is leading to Jesus' Second Coming.

History is linear. That means it has a beginning and an end. Jesus came to earth once as a baby–as the incarnate Son of God. Is that the only time Jesus is coming to earth? No! The Bible teaches us that, in the future, Jesus is coming a second time.

Listen to the writer of Hebrews. **Read Hebrews 9:28.**

**²⁸ so Christ, having been offered once to bear the sins of many, will appear a second time, not to deal with sin but to save those who are eagerly waiting for him.**

What is Jesus going to bring when He comes a second time? **(Allow answers.)** Since He has already dealt with our sins, He is now bringing our ultimate salvation with Him.

Listen to more of God's Word. **Read James 5:7-9.**

**⁷ Be patient, therefore, brothers, until the coming of the Lord. See how the farmer waits for the precious fruit of the earth, being patient about it, until it receives the early and the late rains. ⁸ You also, be patient. Establish your hearts, for the coming of the Lord is at hand. ⁹ Do not grumble against one another, brothers, so that you may not be judged; behold, the Judge is standing at the door.**

---

## *Detail your story...*

**Talk to your child about how having an eye to the Second Coming of Christ changes the way you live your life.**

---

How should the fact that Jesus is coming back again change the way you and I live? **(Allow answers.)** At the very least, it should make us more patient and content!

## *The future ends with our glorification.*

As Christians, we are being sanctified while we await Christ's second coming. But what will happen after that?

Listen. **Read Philippians 3:20-21.**

> [20] **But our citizenship is in heaven, and from it we await a Savior, the Lord Jesus Christ, [21] who will transform our lowly body to be like his glorious body, by the power that enables him even to subject all things to himself.**

Do you know that this is not your home? This world is your temporary home, because Christians belong to heaven. So, Jesus is coming back from heaven to take us there. And then what happens to us? **(Allow answers.)** We receive glorified bodies! We move from justification to sanctification to glorification.

Which leads us to our last truth:

## *The future is life in the new heavens and new earth.*

God is at work making all things new. Remember, everything has been corrupted by sin and death. Jesus is the victor over sin. He is the resurrection and the life. Christians will have a new life with Christ forever!

Listen to these last verses. **Read Revelation 21:1-3.**

> [1] **Then I saw a new heaven and a new earth, for the first heaven and the first earth had passed away, and the sea was no more. [2] And I saw the holy city, new Jerusalem, coming down out of heaven from God, prepared as a bride adorned for her husband. [3] And I heard a loud voice from the throne saying, "Behold, the dwelling place of God is with man. He will dwell with them, and they will be his people, and God himself will be with them as their God."**

What a great way to end! This is your future as a follower of Jesus: Life in the new heaven and new earth, and more importantly, life with God Himself living with us. If you believe in this future, what do you have to worry about in this life? Nothing! Christians have the only hope for the future because it ends in heaven with God!

 DECLARING THE TRUTH

*Lead your child to continue to profess the faith in his or her words:*

*I believe that the Future is...*

- in God's hands.
- about my sanctification.
- leading to the Second Coming of Christ.
- ends with our glorification.
- life in the new heavens and new earth.

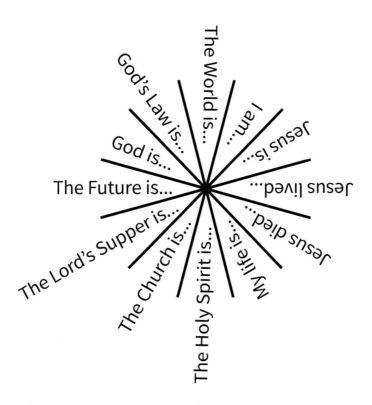

# CONGRATULATIONS!

It is no small feat today to sit down with our young children and have systematic conversations about our faith in Jesus! It is my hope and prayer that, by the work of the Spirit and the Word, your child responds and puts his or her faith in Jesus.

If you believe that has occurred, the next step is to talk with your church leadership about making that profession public. Then, if your child is received as a communing member of your church, the Lord's Supper awaits.

Continue to pray for the salvation of your child so that he or she will be **established in the faith!**

### *About the Author*

## *Dr. John C. Kwasny*

**"You shall teach them [God's commands] diligently to your children, and shall talk of them when you sit in your house, and when you walk by the way, and when you lie down, and when you rise."**

**–Deuteronomy 6:7**

It's an overwhelming responsibility. Life is busy and many things distract us from having those meaningful conversations and equipping our children to experience God by studying His Word. John Kwasny understands. His resources equip parents to share their faith with their children and encourage meaningful discussions that are grounded in deep theology.

God's Word teaches us that the home is to be the primary location of the discipleship of children. As parents, we are called to teach the Scripture to the next generation and to engage with our children in discussions about what it means to love God and embrace Jesus Christ as Savior and Lord. With eight children of his own, Dr. John C. Kwasny understands the struggles parents face. As the Director of Christian Education and Children's Ministry at Pear Orchard Presbyterian Church (PCA) in Ridgeland, Mississippi, John has ministered for over twenty-three years, partnering with parents to disciple the next generation. John has earned an MA in Counseling and a PhD in Christian Education. He is also an adjunct professor at Reformed Theological Seminary (Jackson) and Director of One Story Ministries, authoring children's and youth curriculum for the church, home, and school.